Changes
Beside the Sea

by Liz Gogerly

HODDER
Wayland

an imprint of Hodder Children's Books

Text copyright © 2002 Hodder Wayland

Project manager: Liz Gogerly
Designer: Peta Morey
Picture Research: Shelley Noronha at Glass Onion Pictures
Consultant: Norah Granger

Published in 2002 by Hodder Wayland, an imprint of
Hodder Children's Books

Reprinted in 2003

British Library Cataloguing in Publication Data
Gogerly, Liz
Beside the sea. - (Changes ;1)
1. Holidays - Great Britain - History - 19th century - Juvenile literature
2. Holidays - Great Britain - History - 20th century - Juvenile literature
3. Seaside resorts - Great Britain - History - 19th century - Juvenile literature
4. Seaside resorts - Great Britain - History - 20th century - Juvenile literature
I.Title
394.2'69'146

ISBN 0 7502 3971 9

Printed in
Hong Kong by Wing King Tong

Hodder Children's Books
A division of Hodder Headline Limited
338 Euston Road, London NW1 3BH

PICTURE ACKNOWLEDGEMENTS:
The publisher would like to thank the following for allowing their
pictures to be used in this publication:
Bridgeman Art Library/ Private Collection 10 (top)/ Bonhams, London
14 (top); Mary Evans 4, 9 (top), 15 (top), 18 (top), 19 (top and bottom);
Eye Ubiquitous 18 (bottom); Eyewire (cover);
Hulton Getty (cover and title page), 5 (top), 7 (top), 11 (bottom), 12 (top),
17 (top); Billie Love 6 (top), 8 (top), 16 (top); Popperfoto 5 (bottom),
9 (bottom), 11 (top), 15 (bottom), 17 (bottom); Topham Picturepoint
7 (bottom), 13 (top and bottom); Zul Mukhida 4 (bottom), 6 (bottom),
8 (bottom), 10 (bottom), 12 (bottom), 14 (bottom), 16 (bottom)

While every effort has been made to secure permission, in some cases it
has proved impossible to trace copyright holders.

Contents

Swimming and Paddling

At the seaside it is fun to swim and paddle in the sea. You can swim by yourself or have races. You can splash and play in the waves. Some people have **snorkels** and masks. They can swim underwater and watch the fish. People in the past liked to swim and paddle too.

In **Victorian** times people thought that seawater was good for their health. Many people could not swim. They were rolled out into the sea in **bathing wagons**. Afterwards, they could change into their clothes in the **bathing wagon**.

In the 1920s swimming became **fashionable**. It was fun and it was good exercise. Lots of swimming pools were built next to the sea. These were filled with seawater.

Not everybody wants to get all wet. This couple from the 1940s are happy to paddle at the shore. They watch the children swim and splash about in the water.

Boating and Floating

Surfing the waves on a body board is fun! There are many other ways to float on the water. You can row in a rubber **dinghy**. You can ride in a **pedalo**. You can cut through the waves on a **jet ski**. A long time ago people also enjoyed floating on the sea.

10 RYDE (Isle of Wight). — Arrival of a Steamer. —

Boat trips were popular with the **Victorians** and **Edwardians**. This large boat is called a **steamer**. It carried lots of people. They sailed out to sea and enjoyed the views.

The Lilo was first made in the 1930s. This floating bed bobbed about on the waves. It was new and exciting. These people cannot stop laughing.

These people are enjoying a ride on pedal boats, or **pedalos**. They have to pedal with their feet to make the boat move.

Playing in the Sand

Playing in soft golden sand is great fun. With a bucket and spade you can build a giant castle. Then, you can knock it down and start again! You can dig a hole and fill it with seawater. Children in the past liked to play in the sand as well.

These **Victorian** children have decorated their castle with seaweed. Can you see their bucket and spade? They are made from metal and wood.

Many children like to make boats and cars in the sand. These boys and girls have made a boat. They pretend their spades are the **oars**.

It is a good joke to bury people in sand. This man from the 1950s is buried to his knees. He would have been shocked when the water woke him up.

Fun on the Beach

Playing frisbee is a great beach game. When the sea goes out there is lots of room to play. Football, **volleyball** and tennis are other favourite games. Flying kites and skimming stones are fun too. In the past, children did many of the same things that we do today.

Punch and Judy is a seaside tradition. The funny puppet show makes everyone laugh. In the past, lots of children would gather on the beach to watch the fun and enjoy the jokes.

These girls are playing cricket on the beach. They are wearing their swimming costumes. Do you think they went for a swim after they had finished the game?

Donkey rides have been popular since **Victorian** times. People could choose the donkey they wanted to ride. These children from the 1950s are holding on tightly in case they fall.

Taking the Sea Air

On sunny days you can see lots of people sitting on deck-chairs and sunbeds on the beach. It is relaxing and some people hope they might get a sun-tan. Many years ago people went to the seaside because they thought the clean air was good for their health.

The **Victorians** loved to walk and enjoy the sea air. They built **promenades** next to the sea. These people are **strolling** along the **promenade** and watching other people go by.

Cycling along the **promenade** is another way of breathing in the sea air. These women in the 1940s have hired bicycles for two people. Today we can hire scooters and **Rollerblades** too.

The **Victorians** built piers that we still use today. This photograph of a pier was taken in the 1960s. Can you see the people enjoying the view?

Summer Clothes

The **Victorians** would be shocked if they saw the swimming costumes we wear today. They thought their bodies should be covered. Today, the **fashion** for a sun-tan means swimming costumes have got smaller and smaller. We protect ourselves with sun-glasses and sun-cream.

This painting shows a group of **Victorian** people on the beach. The women and girls wear dresses. The men and boys wear trousers and jackets. Everyone wears a hat to shade them from the sun.

By **Edwardian** times people were wearing quite **daring** swimming costumes. Some of these women are showing their legs! Many costumes were navy-blue and white like a sailor's uniform.

This boy from the 1950s is wearing swimming trunks. The woman wears a one-piece swimming costume. At that time, many people thought it was too daring to wear a **bikini**.

Seaside Snacks

There are lots of treats to eat at the seaside. Ice lollies and ice-creams cool you down. You can buy rock, candyfloss and doughnuts. Some people like fish and chips or burgers. We have so much choice but what did people in the past eat beside the sea?

In **Victorian** times lots of people took a picnic to the beach. This group has two big baskets of food. What do you think they ate?

This photograph from 1939 shows an ice-cream man. In those days some ice-cream sellers had **cool-boxes** for their ices. They sold the ices on the beach.

In the past seafood was a popular snack at the seaside. Cockles, winkles or mussels were a real treat. This boy from the 1940s enjoys his cockles with vinegar.

All the Fun of the Fair

Lots of seaside resorts have a fair. You can ride a bumper car, a merry-go-round or even a roller-coaster. If you are lucky you might win a teddy bear in a **side-show**. People have always enjoyed the fair on holiday. Some of the rides have got much scarier. Many have stayed the same.

This fair in Blackpool began in **Victorian** times. There are merry-go-rounds and a big wheel. These were all powered by steam. The helter-skelter and **side-shows** were great fun too.

These children from the 1930s are riding racing cars. These were powered by electricity. The children are steering themselves. They have to be careful not to crash.

This man in the 1950s is punching the ball as hard as he can. A **scoreboard** tells him how hard he punched. There is no prize in this **side-show** – it is just for fun.

Notes for Parents and Teachers

Changes and the National Curriculum

The books in this series have been chosen so that children can learn more about the way of life of people in the past. Titles such as *A Bite to Eat, Beside the Sea, Dressing Up, Home Sweet Home, School Days* and *Toys and Games* present children with subjects they already know about from their own experiences of life. As such these books may be enjoyed at home or in school, as they satisfy a number of requirements for the Programme of Study for history at Key Stage 1.

These books combine categories from 'Knowledge, skills and understanding' and 'Breadth of study' as required by the National Curriculum. In each spread, the photographs are presented in chronological order. The first photograph is a modern picture that the child should recognize. The following pictures are all historical. Where possible, a wide variety of pictures, including paintings, posters, artefacts and advertisements have been selected. In this way children can see the different ways in which the past is represented. A lively selection of pictures also helps to develop the children's skills of observation. In turn, this will encourage them to ask questions and discuss their own ideas.

The text is informative and raises questions for the children to talk about in class or at home. It is supported by further information about the historical photographs (see right). Once the children are familiar with the photographs you could ask them to guess when the pictures were taken – if it isn't mentioned in the text. By looking at clues such as clothes, hairstyles, style of buildings and vehicles they might be able to make reasonable guesses. There are further questions to ask your child or class on the right.

About the Photos

Swimming and Paddling
Pages 4–5

A magazine cover from 1893 of a bathing wagon.
Questions to ask:
- Why do you think there is a rope?
- Do you think their swimming costumes were comfortable?

Crowds posing beside the swimming pool, or lido, in Margate, Kent in 1929.
Questions to ask:
- What are the people standing on?
- What are the men wearing as swimming costumes?

An elderly couple paddling at Whitley Bay in 1948.
Question to ask:
- Why are some people in the water wearing rubber hats?

Boating and Floating
Pages 6–7

A postcard from 1910 showing the arrival of a steamer at the Isle of Wight.
Questions to ask:
- Why do you think the boat was called a steamer?
- Why do you think the women have umbrellas?

Bathers at Margate enjoying the new craze for Lilos in 1934.
Question to ask:
- Can you see anything besides the Lilos that are made from rubber?

Boating at Butlins Holiday Camp in Filey in 1946.
Questions to ask:
- What are the boats made from?
- Have you been on a pedalo? Did it look like this?

Playing in the Sand
Pages 8–9

Children making sandcastles on the Isle of Wight in 1900.
Questions to ask:
- Do you think the children feel comfortable in these clothes?
- Can you see what the children have stuck into their sandcastle?

Children making a sand boat in 1923.
Question to ask:
- Can you tell by looking at this picture if it was a sunny day?

A man being covered in sand at Bournemouth in 1952.
Questions to ask:
- What has the man got on his head?
- What are the children's beach toys made from?

Fun on the Beach
Pages 10–11

An illustration by Molly Benatar from a children's annual called *Blackies*, *circa* 1920–1940.
Questions to ask:
- Do you know the name of the puppet sitting at the front of the puppet theatre?
- Can you tell by looking at the children's clothes when this picture was painted?

Girls playing cricket on a beach on the north-east coast in 1934.
Question to ask:
- Can you think of other games that people play on the beach?

Holidaymakers in Blackpool in 1955 enjoying the donkeys.
Questions to ask:
- Do you know the name of the tower in the background?
- Can you see the names of the donkeys?

Taking the Sea Air
Pages 12–13

A view of Scarborough in North Yorkshire at the beginning of the twentieth century.
Questions to ask:
- Do you think people felt hot in their clothes?
- Do people still like to walk on promenades now?

Women riding tandem bicycles at Clacton, *circa* 1939.
Question to ask:
- Can you see a pier in this picture?

Brighton Pier in the 1960s.
Questions to ask:
- Can you see any attractions on the pier?
- What do you think the couple to the right of the picture are eating?

Summer Clothes
Pages 14–15

Painting of a family on the shores of Bognor Regis by Alexander Rossi (1870–1903).
Questions to ask:
- Do you think any of these people would have swam in the sea?
- What do you think some of the people are drinking?

Holidaymakers wearing swimming costumes in 1911.
Questions to ask:
- Do you think these swimming costumes were comfortable?
- Why do you think these people were so covered up?

Playing on Bournemouth beach in 1952.
Question to ask:
- Are these swimming costumes similar to yours?

Seaside Snacks
Pages 16–17

A picnic on the Isle of Wight, *circa* 1900.
Questions to ask:
- What kinds of food would you take on a picnic to the beach?
- What do you think Victorian people drank beside the sea?

An ice-cream seller in the sea at Brighton in 1939.
Question to ask:
- Do you see ice-cream sellers like this on your holidays?

At the shellfish stall at Southend in 1948.
Questions to ask:
- Do you think the boy likes the cockles?
- Do you think it is a hot day?

All the Fun of the Fair
Pages 18–19

Blackpool Pleasure Beach in 1915.
Questions to ask:
- Can you see any seaside snacks for sale?
- Which rides do you know in this photograph?

The 'Monte Carlo Rally' electric car ride at Dreamland Amusement Park, Margate in 1938.
Questions to ask:
- Who is winning the race?
- Can you see the bumpers around the cars? What were they for?

A side-show on a pier in the 1950s.
Question to ask:
- Do you think the young boy would like a go too?

Glossary

bathing wagon A wooden hut on wheels that was pulled out to sea by horses. Swimmers could change into their bathing costumes inside the hut.

bikini A swimming costume with two parts worn by females.

cool-box A container with a special lining that helps to keep cold food and drinks cool.

daring Bold and quite shocking.

dinghy A small, open rowing boat, often made from rubber.

Edwardian Used to describe anything from the time of King Edward VII (1901–1910).

fashion/ fashionable A style of dressing, or way of doing things that becomes popular at a certain time.

jet ski A small motor vehicle that looks like a scooter. It is steered with handlebars and rides across water.

oar A wooden pole with a flat blade at one end. Two oars or more are used to row a boat.

pedalo A small boat with pedals to make it go.

promenade A paved road or path that runs along the seafront.

Rollerblades Boots with wheels attached to them, used for rolling or moving along.

scoreboard A board showing the number of points scored by a player in a game.

side-show A small show or game at a fair.

snorkel A plastic tube for breathing through when you are swimming underwater.

steamer A large boat that has an engine powered by steam. Coal or wood is burned to boil water. The steam from the water makes the engine work.

stroll To walk slowly.

Victorian Used to describe anything from the time when Queen Victoria ruled Britain (1837–1901).

volleyball A game where players use their hands to hit a ball over a net to score points.

Further Information

Books to Read
Non-fiction
At the Seaside by D. Church
(Franklin Watts, 2000)

Fiction
Iggy Pig at the Seaside
by Vivian French
(Hodder Children's Books, 1999)
Mulberry Alone at the Seaside
by Sally Grindley
(Hodder Wayland, 1999)
Seaside Poems edited by
Jill Bennett
(Oxford University Press, 1998)

Sources
Beside the Seaside
by Joseph Connolly
(Octopus Publishing, 1999)
*Sun, Fun and Crowds: Seaside
Holidays Between the Wars*
by Steven Braggs and Diane Harris
(Tempus, 2000)

Websites
*http://home.freeuk.com/elloughton
13/seaconte.htm*
This site has lots of activities and
information about the seaside. Join
a family on a daytrip to Blackpool.
Look at Blackpool from the top of
the tower. Make your own beach
picture. Find more old photographs
of people having fun beside the
seaside a long time ago.

Website for Teachers
*http://www.standards.dfes.gov.uk/
schemes/history/?version=1*
Look for the unit 'What were
seaside holidays like in the past?'
It suggests useful ideas for teaching
this subject to year 1 and 2 pupils.

Index